Diary of a Serial App Developer
Revised and Illustrated Edition

Mark Carlotto

Preface

I wasn't one of those people waiting in line all night for an iPhone in 2007. I had a flip phone and liked it. It worked and was easy to use. A year later as its popularity grew, I bought an iPhone not for the reasons most people wanted it, for email, the web, camera, music, etc., but to develop apps. I saw the iPhone as a computer you could put in your pocket that had an internet connection, a user interface, and a bunch of cool sensors including a camera, microphone, and GPS. New technology and the freedom of creating and selling my own ideas inspired me to become an app developer. It was more than fun – it was addicting. One idea led to another – to over a hundred apps in less than ten years. This is the story of how I got started, what I've done, and why I've done it.

Table of Contents

Figure 1 Fall 2008 iPhone TV commercial that showed my first app, *Pitch to Note*.

Instant Gratification

Nothing is out of the question for me. I'm always thinking about creating. My future starts when I wake up in the morning and see the light... Then I'm grateful. – Miles Davis

I was a rock-and-roll drummer in high school and wanted to major in music. I also liked science. "Good drummers are a dime a dozen," my dad said and convinced me to pursue a career in science and engineering. I started college as a physics major, dropped out at the end of my sophomore year, and got a job. Becoming interested in electronic music, I began to build a synthesizer and soon realized that I was more of an engineer than a scientist at heart. I went back to school a year later and changed my major from physics to electrical engineering. After graduation, I got a job in the aerospace industry. As my interests evolved from electronic music and signal processing to image processing, pattern recognition, remote sensing, and mapping, the synthesizer I started to build was forgotten.

Over time I started playing flute and piano. Now, years later, I am thinking about developing music apps and have an idea that uses the iPhone's built-in microphone to detect musical notes and display them on the screen. My ear for pitch is not as good as my sense of rhythm. With a pitch detector, I would know what others are playing without having to ask about notes, chords, etc. – sort of like having a musical aid. Seems like the sort of gadget others might buy.

September 2008

I finally bought an iPhone and started working on my music app. A lot of signal-processing algorithms operate in the frequency domain. I thought about using a Fast Fourier Transform (FFT) to convert an audio signal into its spectrum but discovered that FFTs are way too compute-intensive for the iPhone. After all, it is just a phone. Instead, I implemented a bank of recursive filters using fixed-point arithmetic. Each filter is tuned to a musical pitch from A0, the lowest note on a piano keyboard, to C8, the highest note. When a note is played, the corresponding filter lights up. The display is kind of geeky – a bar graph showing the response from the filter bank – but it works. I think I'm going to try to sell it on iTunes.

October 2008

Apple approved my pitch detection app, which I named *Pitch to Note*. My daughter was watching TV a few nights ago and said, "Hey Dad, I think I saw your app on an iPhone commercial just now." A little later it played again, and sure enough, there it was.[1] It was kind of amazing – in one month I paid $99 to become an app developer, created my first app, saw it advertised on TV, and started making a little money on the side.

Pitch to Note is great for tuning a guitar but is not the best kind of display for a musician. With a little more work, I turned the bar graph into musical notation by mapping detected pitches to notes on a musical staff. I created a new app called *Pitch to Note +* *Chord* that also detects chords using a pattern recognition algorithm I invented. The algorithm compares detected notes against all possible chord types in all keys and picks the chord with the best match.[2] Where my first app looked like a science experiment, *Pitch to Note +* looks like something a musician might actually use.[3]

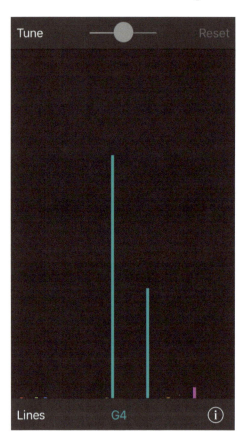

Figure 2 *Pitch to Note* (left) and *Pitch to Note + Chord* (right).

[1] https://youtu.be/-sncCSbPlUw?t=93
[2] Mark Carlotto, "Continuous Real-Time Determination of Key and Chords in Live Music Using Minimum Description Length," Available at SSRN: https://ssrn.com/abstract=3507004
[3] https://www.youtube.com/watch?v=rYyvTHR02VQ

November 2008

In the early 1970s, I worked on an undergraduate research project to design a digital music synthesizer. Analog instruments like the Moog synthesizer were very popular at the time. The digital approach is based on something called additive synthesis, which involves generating lots of simple sine waves and adding them up to create complex tones. It was a computationally intensive way of generating electronic music. At around the same time, John Chowning at Stanford came up with a different approach based on frequency modulation or FM that was later adopted by musical instrument manufacturers like Yamaha and Korg. In contrast to the computational complexity of additive synthesis, FM uses a few simple oscillators to create really complex and interesting musical timbres with a minimal amount of effort. The idea appealed to me – after all why work harder than you have to?

I'd like to develop an FM synth for the iPhone, but the device is so small I can't imagine someone actually playing it. So instead of something you play, I think it might be interesting to create an app that uses a pitch detector to feed notes into a synthesizer. The app would in effect "follow" the notes it hears.

Sound from Sound Synth is selling but has a couple of problems. First, is the latency or delay between the time the pitch detector first recognizes a note to when the synth plays it. Electrons moving through an analog circuit at the speed of light have no detectable delay. Latency is, however, a problem with any digital device that processes data by a series of programmed operations (e.g., adds, multiplies, etc.) The iPhone processes audio in chunks, typically about 1K (1024) samples. The iOS operating system buffers chunks so that they can be processed in real-time. At a standard audio sampling rate of 44,100 Hz, three 1K buffers result in a time delay of about 70 milliseconds, which is noticeable.

The second problem with the app is feedback. Let's say you are playing something on the piano. The microphone picks up the music, the pitch detector sends the notes to the synth, and the synth plays the notes through the iPhone's speaker, which are picked up by the microphone creating a feedback loop. If you put on a pair of headphones to avoid feedback, the synth follows what you're playing but with an annoying delay. Not sure where to go with this app so I'm putting it on the back burner for a while.

December 2008

My wife and I live north of Boston on Cape Ann. Like Cape Cod, Cape Ann is best known for its seacoast. Less known is a deserted colonial village in the middle of the Cape known as Dogtown. Soon after moving here a few years ago, I got lost hiking in the woods of Dogtown and decided to map it. Part of what I do for a living involves satellite imaging so mapping Dogtown seemed like a reasonable thing to do. In my free time, I spent many hours hiking and exploring, mapping trails, stone walls, cellar holes, and other features using a handheld GPS and some home-grown Mac software for displaying tracks and waypoints on a map background. In 2007 I published a map and book called *The Dogtown Guide.*[4]

I'm using Google Earth to create a new digital map of Dogtown that combines ground photos with overhead imagery and discovered a cool feature called a photo overlay. When you click on a photo overlay, Google Earth zooms into the photo in such a way that you're viewing it in the context in which it was taken. Aside from some demo photos I found on the web, I wondered how to make my own photo overlays. The iPhone with its camera, GPS, and most recent addition, a magnetometer for determining heading, seems like the perfect device for capturing photo overlays. This month I released a new app called *Photo-Overlay Tool*. Despite its terrible name and even worse design (you can't see the photo you've taken until you download it to your computer), a surprising number of people have bought the app.

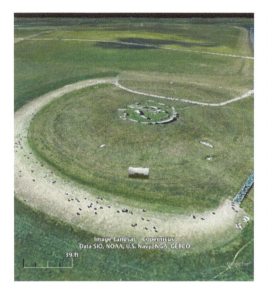

Figure 3 Photo-overlay taken at Stonehenge.

January 2009

Getting an app to work can take a while. When it's finally done, I'm ready to move on to something else, something completely different. Getting back to music, I have an idea for an app that tells you the key of a song in real time. Since *Pitch to Note* gives us the notes, all we need is a way to determine the key from the notes. So I thought of an algorithm where notes "vote" for musical keys; e.g., a C natural might vote for the keys

---

[4] Mark Carlotto, *The Dogtown Guide*, Lulu Press, 2008, 2017; Kindle, 2016.

of C, F, G, and so forth because those keys have a C natural in them, but not, say, for the keys of D, A, and E, which do not. As a song plays and notes are processed, the correct key emerges as the one with the most votes. The algorithm uses what's called a "lossy integrator" that adds up votes for keys from recent notes and forgets votes from old notes. In this way, the app can track key changes over time. I plot the relative number of votes for all keys on a bar graph displayed over a piano keyboard. Again, not the most inspired user interface. As a song modulates from one key to another the bar graph changes accordingly. *What Key*[5] was approved for sale early this month and has been doing well despite a few complaints that the app jumps around from key to key, which is strange because that is what most songs do.

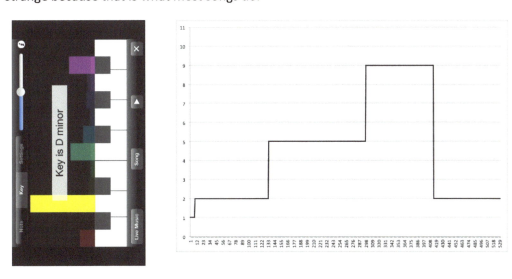

Figure 4 *What Key* app (left) and key vs. time plot for Bach's *Invention in D minor* (right).

In the process of developing *What Key,* I made some improvements to the pitch detector, which is also used in *Pitch to Note* and *Sound from Sound Synth.* I simplified the FM synth in *Sound from Sound Synth* and built a new app called *Resonizer.* The app has less latency but still suffers from feedback issues. Although it can generate some "interesting" sound effects, anticipating bad reviews from unsuspecting users, I eventually removed the *Resonizer* from iTunes.

February 2009

I have this pattern going of developing a music app or two and then switching to a mapping/navigation app. I've been hiking quite a bit and am thinking about an app for taking pictures that can be referenced to a map and annotated – sort of like a travel atlas. I call the app *iAtlas*. Like the iPhone's camera app, *iAtlas* stores pictures in a camera roll. A map window shows where each picture in the roll was taken, and an

---

[5] https://www.youtube.com/watch?v=CAWqbZ3ISgw

editable text window lets you add short descriptions. Where I had been taking a picture with the camera, adding a waypoint on the GPS, and jotting down a few comments in a notebook, I can now use *iAtlas* to do all three at the same time. *iAtlas* is also my first app to communicate with what is becoming known as the "cloud," allowing you to post and share geo-referenced pictures on a website.[6]

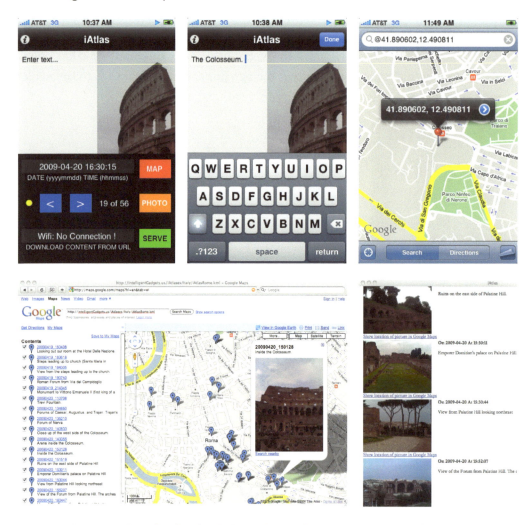

Figure 5 *iAtlas* screenshots (top), uploaded KML file displayed in Google Earth (bottom left) and webpage (bottom right).

March 2009

I write code but am not a software engineer. I use any and every means to code up an idea. Usually, I start with something I've already developed and modify it – cut and paste one section of code from this app, another section from that app, etc. I try to avoid writing anything from scratch. Open source is good, but websites such as Stack

---

[6] https://youtu.be/5OWKvm4kxlM

Overflow with code snippets are great. I'd probably still be developing my first app if it wasn't for all the help that's out there on the internet. That said, there's a lot of wrong information too, which can get you hopelessly lost.

The mechanics of developing an app is easy if you can code and know your way around the Mac and iOS operating systems. I use a language called Objective C – a dialect of the C programming language, which was developed by researchers at Bell Labs in 1972. Apps are developed within a programming environment called Xcode where you code up the application, create a user interface (UI), add resources the app requires such as sound files and images, and so on. The complete software package is uploaded to iTunes. There you add information about the app (metadata) including pictures and links to demos. Apple reviews your submission. If they find a problem, the app is rejected, and you go back and fix it. When it is finally approved, the app appears on iTunes. So far, I've developed about a half-dozen apps in as many months and have been averaging about 30 app sales per day.

April 2009

My wife is an art teacher. Between the two of us and our kids, there are always a lot of ideas floating around. She has been using an Eastern motif known as a mandala to teach art and meditation. It occurred to me that a mandala might be a nice metaphor for a different kind of musical instrument. I found an image of a mandala consisting of a pattern of eight circles around a larger circle. The shape was not unlike an instrument called a hang drum – a metal percussion instrument that is tuned to a fixed scale. I decided on a design for a new instrument where the circles are touch-sensitive pads, each tuned to a note in a scale. I used the FM synth I had already developed as the sound engine. What makes the instrument, which I call *Mandala Music*, cool is that the scales, notes, and even the sound can be changed. The best part is that they're no wrong notes, anything you play sounds great.

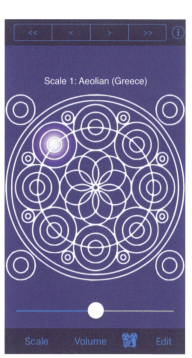

Figure 6 *Mandala Music*[7]

My wife, who cringes at the sound of some of my other apps, loves *Mandala Music*.

---

[7] https://youtu.be/ZxBAqT3jtVs

May 2009

A few years ago, my family put together a cookbook of Italian recipes from the *Marche* region of Italy. My dad self-published the cookbook under the supervision of my mom and aunts. Just returning from a trip to Italy I thought it would be useful to create an app that finds recipes in the cookbook based on available ingredients. Say you have some pasta, garlic, and olive oil. What can I make? After years of my dad telling me to cut the grass and rake the leaves, I decided to put him to work converting the family recipes into XML – extensible markup language. In response to what you have, the app tells you what you can make in the cookbook. I implemented *What to Eat?* in another language called PHP. *What to Eat?* is a web app[8] so my relatives who don't own iPhones but have computers and internet can use it.

June 2009

After setting up a web service I realized you could do other things besides serving up Italian recipes. This month I released a free social media app called *iBlat* that lets you post a picture with a message at your geographic location.[9] It is a way of sharing information geographically. Clicking on a link takes you to a website that shows messages from people who are nearby.

At work, my boss asked me to come up with a demo for a GEOINT trade show. GEOINT, which stands for geospatial intelligence, can be almost anything about the earth's surface including what's on it. I thought an app like *iBlat* might be a good way of collecting and posting GEOINT reports. My two creative universes – developing algorithms during the day and apps at night – were starting to overlap. I was beginning to wonder if other apps I was starting to think about might apply to projects at work and so decided to ask my boss if the company was interested in them. App development was fun, but I didn't want to run the risk of losing my job over it.

July 2009

Inventing a key algorithm or piece of code that can be used over and over again is important in app development. Without code reuse, each new project starts from scratch and has no connection with other projects. Plus, bug fixes and improvements to one piece of code benefit all the apps that use it.

The pitch detector I developed for *Pitch to Note* is a key algorithm that has been used in several apps. This month, I'm using it in a new app called *Audio to MIDI Recorder* to convert live audio into MIDI data. Musical instrument digital interface or MIDI is the

---

[8] https://intelligentgadgets.us/wte/wteItalian.php

[9] *iBlat* was created three years before Facebook went public in May 2012.

standard by which electronic musical instruments communicate with one another and is a common interchange format. If you go online, you can probably find a .mid file for just about any song that someone has sequenced (converted) by hand. I'd like to develop an app that can sequence or transcribe music automatically from audio to MIDI. *Audio to MIDI* works pretty well with solo instruments but fails miserably on music with multiple instruments, vocals, and percussion. Although I have made some improvements to the pitch detector, I am beginning to realize, mostly from a lot of negative iTunes reviews, that automatic music transcription is a hard problem. Perhaps that's why nobody else seems to be doing it.

 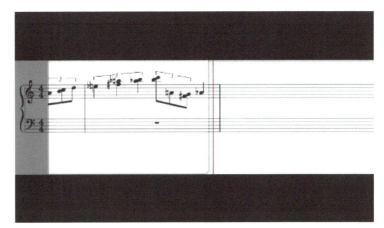

Figure 7 *Audio to MIDI Recorder* running on live music (left). Playback of recorded MIDI file using Garage Band (right).

August 2009

Towards the end of the summer, I developed an app that displays images from NASA's Blue Marble database over any place on Earth. The app shows large-scale features such as Mount Everest and the Grand Canyon in 3D. The effect of depth is created by texture mapping Blue Marble images onto a digital elevation model, which is downloaded along with the imagery. Computer graphics rendering code running on the iPhone generates synthetic images from different look directions that are superimposed and viewed with red and blue anaglyphic glasses. Although rendering is fairly compute-intensive, the time it takes to generate a 3D image is negligible to the time it takes to download the data from the cloud. I'm beginning to realize that communication is the limiting factor in mobile devices, not the devices themselves.[10]

---

[10] https://youtu.be/9YOEEpWAXgU

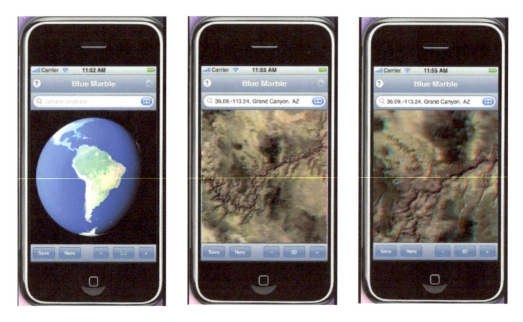

Figure 8 *Blue Marble* app could display 1 km/pixel 3D images anywhere in the world.

Minimum Viable Product

It's weird. They always travel in groups of five. These programmers, there's always a tall skinny white guy, a short skinny Asian guy, fat guy with a ponytail, some guy with crazy facial hair and then an East Indian guy. It's like they trade guys until they all have the right group. – Gavin Belson, *Silicon Valley*[11]

The instant gratification of making and selling apps was starting to become a business. But there weren't five guys, it was just me. I am coming up with the ideas, writing code, designing UIs, making promotional videos, and more. I am doing it all (or at least trying). After one year as an iPhone developer, I have over a dozen apps on iTunes with over 1500 units sold. In search of one killer app, I am leaving behind a trail of niche apps. And so, it continues as I begin my second year as a developer.

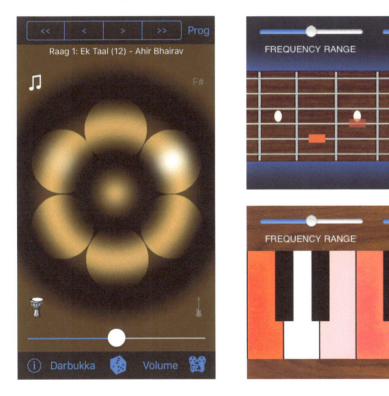

Figure 9 Music app spinoffs include *Mantra Music* (left), *Auto Guitar* (top right), and *Enlightened Piano* (bottom right).

---

[11] https://youtu.be/XdGvPUzwYng?si=9SY61wVG06ern2gt

In September, I released *World Drums* in which you can play various drums from around the world using samples from Western drum kits to Middle Eastern dumbeks and Indian tablas. In late October, I created an app called *Mantra Music* that combines *Mandala Music* and *World Drums* with Hindustani musical sequences used in Indian classical music. Early in 2010 came *Auto Guitar* and *Enlightened Piano* – two more spinoffs of *Pitch to Note* technology, which display detected notes from live music onto guitar and piano keyboards. Although I have not solved the latency problem, you can listen to a song and strum or play along provided the changes are not too quick.

Given my newfound appreciation of the communications limitations of mobile technology, I am beginning to rethink geo apps and have some new ideas.

December 2009

Late fall to early winter before the deep cold sets in is the best time to hike in the woods. Over the last couple of months, I have expanded my historical research beyond Dogtown to the whole of the inland woods. When the colonial settlement was abandoned around 1800, some people relocated to the harbor to work maritime trades. Others moved north to mine Cape Ann granite. For hundreds of years, the interior of the Cape was crisscrossed by a network of old roads and footpaths that connected all of these places. I'm trying to locate the original roads by correlating historical maps with the current trail system.

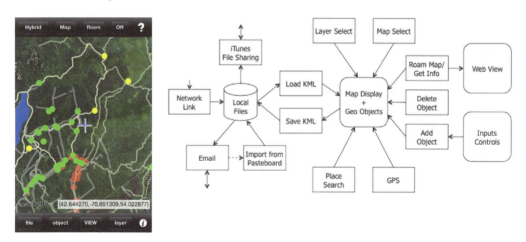

Figure 10 *KML Map* functional architecture design (right) and screenshot (left).

An issue I have with the Google Earth app for the iPhone is that you must store your data in the cloud. I want to be able to take the data with me so that I can use it in places where there is no cell service and hence no cloud to communicate with. Starting with last year's *Photo Overlay Tool*, I wrote a basic KML file reader, added a map display, and UI to make a new app called *KML* Map that lets you store data on the phone. Map data are represented using keyhole markup language or KML for short. KML was developed for Google Earth, originally called Keyhole Earth Viewer, by a company called Keyhole, Inc., which was later acquired by Google. KML is complicated and so implementing an app that can deal with all its intricacies was out of the question. Instead, I've implemented what's called a "minimum viable product." *KML Map* supports basic map features such as placemarks, line strings, polygons, and image and photo overlays. As people buy the app they ask if I can add this or that feature. And so each update has some new capability such as KMZ (compressed KML) files, tracks, multi-geometry objects, embedded HTML, network links, and more. A problem with this kind of incremental development is that software evolution is not pretty and leads to code that can be hard to understand and maintain.

January 2010

A few months ago at my mother-in-law's condo, our niece told us that she had had some weird paranormal experiences one night. The previous summer, her mother said that they saw a UFO that looked like a hotel floating over Long Island. I thought it might be interesting to develop an app to detect these kinds of phenomena. One researcher I know discovered that UFOs can cause changes in magnetic fields.[12] I decided to explore a new iOS sensor framework and API that deals with the iPhone's magnetometer. The magnetometer is what's used in compass apps to determine heading – the direction you're facing relative to north. Instead of using the x-y-z components of the magnetic field to find north, I developed an anomaly detection algorithm that triggers an alarm when there are changes in its direction or magnitude. I don't know if *MAD*, which stands

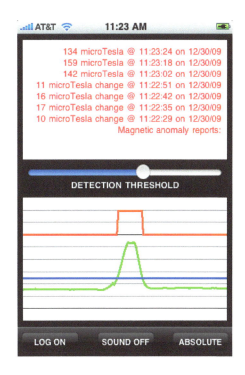

Figure 11 *Magnetic Anomaly Detector* (*MAD*) generates an alarm when the magnetic flux density exceeds a preset threshold.

for *Magnetic Anomaly Detector* has actually detected the presence of a UFO or a ghost, but it can detect nails in walls and works great as a stud finder (provided there's a nail close by).

---

[12] Maccabee, B., "Strong Magnetic Field Detected Following a Sighting of and Unidentified Flying Object," *Journal of Scientific Exploration* 8, 347 (1994)

February 2010

More than a diversion, *MAD* revealed the potential of the iPhone as a sophisticated sensor, which suggests some new applications. A few years ago, I read William Gibson's novel *Spook Country* in which he talks about something called locative art. The basic concept involves viewing virtual art objects in space. I thought of something simpler – why not develop an app that displays map icons and geo-referenced photos (i.e., photo overlays) floating around you in space instead of on a map? *AR Viewer* is my first attempt at augmented reality (AR). The app displays a KML file containing placemarks, line strings, polygons, and photo overlays as objects that appear in the camera view of the device. Objects within the field of view of the camera that are in front of you are visible. Closer objects appear larger. Objects behind you are only visible if you turn around and aim the iPhone in their direction.

Figure 12 *AR Viewer* displays KML objects in the iPhone's camera view.

After implementing the app, it is clear that the iPhone has some serious limitations with respect to AR. Magnetometer errors affect the direction the object appears. If the compass freezes (not an uncommon occurrence), the AR view freezes. GPS accuracy limits how close a virtual object can be from the device. If you are too close to an object, the location error can place the object you are looking for behind you.

We started to play around with some AR ideas at work. I put together a demo that takes a satellite image, finds objects like military vehicles, generates a KML file, and displays the objects using *AR Viewer*. It was a cool idea, but the demos never really worked that well because of the device issues. Once, when I was walking around the DC area holding up my phone to look at some virtual objects, I was approached by a security guard, who wanted to know what I was doing. It took a while to explain, but eventually, he let me go and suggested that I take my experiments elsewhere.

The company was becoming interested in mobile technology but not the iPhone, perhaps for the same reasons why they preferred PC to Mac. They told me I was free to do my own thing, on my own time.

March 2010

A few months ago, Apple emailed developers encouraging them to submit apps for the upcoming iPad. I decided to finally make the synthesizer I had dreamed of building back in my college days. The design starts with what I had developed for *Mandala Music,* adds another oscillator, and enhances the envelope generators. FM synths are very economical in generating a lot of sound with a little computation but can be hard to program. For example, let's say we have two oscillators running at frequencies f_1 and f_2. Using just a couple of table lookups, multiplies, and adds, FM generates as many sum and difference frequencies $nf_1 \pm mf_2$ as you like depending on a control parameter called the modulation index. Increasing the modulation index is like sweeping the lowpass filter in an analog synthesizer. I designed the control settings to limit the choice of modulating frequencies to produce only harmonic overtones of the fundamental frequency, i.e., *f, 2f, 3f,...* Non-harmonic overtones are cool but can get kind of weird.

I have prototype code running in an interim app for the iPhone called *Synthia. Synthia* has a variable-size piano keyboard and a portamento control for gliding between notes. Portamento was a cool feature of early analog synthesizers that I always liked. With three oscillators and matching envelope generators, my new synth can generate a much wider range of timbres including woodwinds, brass, and strings. *Synthia* is not an easy instrument to play (unless you have very small fingers) but it sounds really good for something you can carry around in your pocket.

Figure 13 *SynSurface* with two FM oscillators per key was my first iPad app.

April 2010

Just after the iPad was released, Apple approved the full-up version of my synth. Unlike *Synthia*, *SynSurface* has a much larger screen with all the controls laid out and a keyboard that you can play. Unfortunately, no one seems to be buying it. Established names in the musical instrument business are releasing their apps, which look and sound a lot better. After all, they've been in the business for years. Still, I am encouraged to keep at it. Besides creating revolutionary devices like the iPhone and iPad, Apple has developed an equally revolutionary and democratic process for developing and selling apps. It's a level playing field where everyone, from large well-established companies to first-time developers, can participate.

 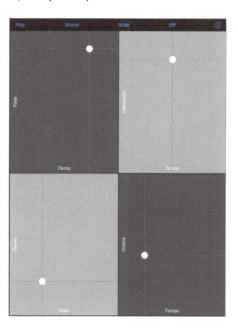

Figure 14 *Mandala Music HD* play screen (left) and internal synthesizer control (right).

Summer 2010

Instead of trying to compete with the big boys, I have decided to focus on what I do best. Late in the spring, I released *Mandala Music HD,* an enhanced iPad version of *Mandala Music* with some cool auto-looping features.[13] There seems to be no limit to what you can do with these devices. I've come up with some new drum apps based on looping concepts. *Drum Circle Jam*[14] is *World Drums* with a looper. After setting the tempo and meter (beats per measure) the looper records a measure of what you've played and plays it back. You can quantize and clean up what you've played, add

---

[13] https://www.youtube.com/watch?v=hH8IVArPYcM
[14] https://youtu.be/5uYyLtDOmDo

additional loops, change tempo, and even the meter (e.g., from 4/4 to 3/4 time).

With another new app, *Drum-O-Rama,* you can build your own custom drum sets from a selection of over a hundred samples – Western drums, cymbals, and percussion sounds from all over the world. Drums can be played manually or can trigger a beat sequencer programmed for that drum. For example, tapping a ride cymbal can trigger the traditional "ding, ding-a-ding, ding-a-ding" jazz pattern, which loops while you play snare, toms, and bass drum.[15]

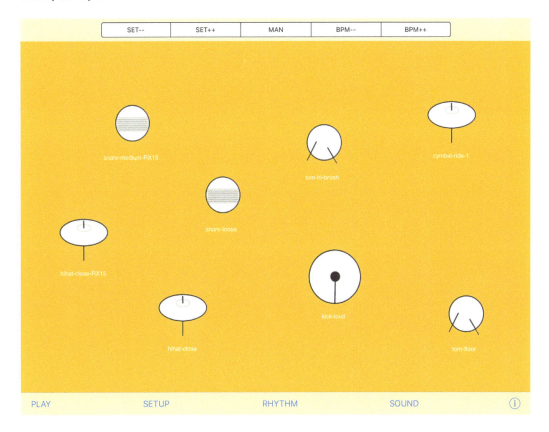

Figure 15 iPad version of *Drum-O-Rama.*

Fall 2010

Going from synthesis to analysis, I've developed a new app called *MUSYS* that combines the pitch and chord detectors in *Pitch to Note +* with scale and key models in *What Key* to analyze a song in terms of its notes, chords, scales, and key. Although the app is selling, some users do not like it. One reviewer said the display looked as if someone had "thrown up" on the screen. Like a few of my other apps, *MUSYS* is a work in progress.

---

[15] https://youtu.be/PVq9CmL2mXQ

Other apps worth mentioning as I conclude my second year of development include *GeoTagger* which records your location and posts it to a web server so people can track you on Google Earth, and two eBook apps – *Exploring Dogtown*, a collection of maps, and other resources from *The Dogtown Guide*, and *Martian Enigmas*,[16] which is based on a book I published a few years ago.

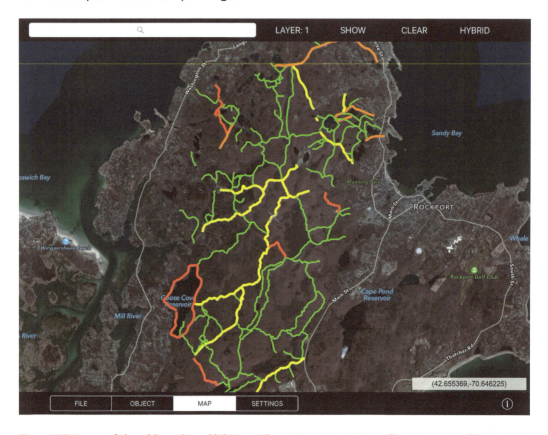

Figure 16 A map of the old roads and hiking trails on Cape Ann, Massachusetts created using *KML Map HD*, an iPad version of *KML Map*.

---

[16] Mark Carlotto, *The Martian Enigmas: A Closer Look*, North Atlantic Books, 1991, 1993; Kindle, 2016.

Addictive Development

> The key to building a high quality, robust, and addictive app that resonates well with end users is to explicitly approach the developing, testing, launching, marketing, and selling of the app with the intention of creating an in-demand product within a hungry market that solves a pressing customer pain and organically encourages viral and habitual engagement. – Appster[17]

Instead of building apps that are addictive to users, I find myself addicted to the development process itself. I can't seem to stop developing apps. One idea leads to another. They all seem good. Last year, I tripled the number of apps and increased sales more than 10x to almost 18,000 units. At the beginning of my third year of app development, I created an eBook version of a children's story that my wife wrote and illustrated called *Through the Stars*. I am also developing some alternative camera apps.

I've always been interested in 3D photography. 3D photos are simply two photos – one for each eye – that create the impression of depth when viewed together. Normally you need a special camera with two lenses to take a 3D photo. Another way to do it is to point a regular camera at a subject, take a picture, move a short distance, and take a second picture. Once the photos are aligned, objects that are closer to the camera appear to have more parallax or left-right shifts than objects that are farther away. Viewing the photos side-by-side or with a special viewer, objects closer to the camera seem to pop out of the image.

My first 3D app called *EZ 3-D Photo*[18] takes a 3D picture by simply pointing and swiping the iPhone left to right (or right to left). While working on *EZ 3-D Photo* I realized that you could make 3D videos the same way by using the motion of the camera, or the motion of objects relative to the camera, to generate the 3D effect. *3-D Movie Camera* exploits this phenomenon, first used by computer vision researchers in the 1980s for computing structure from motion. While making a 3D movie, the app automatically measures camera motion and renders the movie as two side-by-side frames. If you point the camera out of the side of a moving car, objects closer to you move faster and appear closer to you than objects far away. The faster you move the camera, or objects move relative to the camera, the greater the 3D effect. One of my favorite demos is of

---

[17] https://www.appsterhq.com/blog/build-viral-apps/
[18] https://www.youtube.com/watch?v=qsNFFf8x6DY&t=8s

fish swimming in an aquarium. The greater the horizontal motion of the fish, the more they appear to move in and out of the screen. Objects moving in the principal direction of motion seem to approach the viewer while those moving in the opposite direction recede.

Figure 17 3D photos created by *EZ 3-D Photo* app. To see depth, relax the eyes and gaze at the top photo pair until the vertical and horizontal bars overlap to form a "+".

Winter 2011

Just about everybody knows about *Auto-Tune*, which uses signal processing to change (correct) the pitch of your voice. I've been thinking about an app that uses your voice to control a synth. Deriving pitch information from voice is hard because there isn't a lot of energy in the fundamental and vocal spectra are not harmonic like that of a musical instrument but depend on the shape of the vocal cavity. In fact, it is this shape that determines the sound of your voice. The filter bank developed for *Pitch to Note* correlates the audio signal with a set of pure tones – sine and cosine waves at different frequencies. It works well for musical instruments but not for voice. So instead of correlating the signal with pure tones, I implemented an autocorrelation algorithm that compares the signal with time-delayed versions of itself. The delay d with the highest correlation gives the fundamental frequency $f=1/d$ of your voice. That frequency, converted to a musical pitch and encoded as a MIDI signal, controls a synth. Since the iPhone is not powerful enough to do all of this processing and run a synth at the same time, the MIDI signal is sent wirelessly to a networked computer. I've been testing *MIDI Voice Controller* with *Garage Band* running on a Mac and it works great.

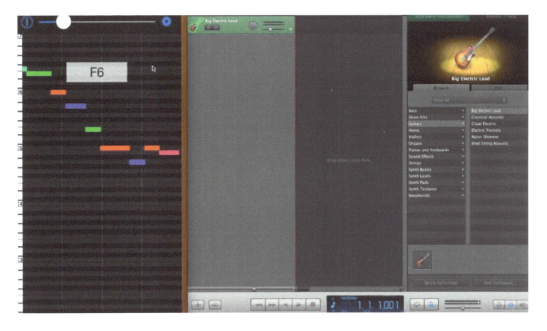

Figure 18 *MIDI Voice Controller* connected to Garage Band.

Spring 2011

I removed *AR Viewer* from iTunes last fall because the 3G's sensors weren't accurate enough for AR. When you held up the phone, features were almost always shifted from where they should be and sometimes were not visible at all because the app put something that you were looking for behind you. With the release of the iPhone 4 with better sensors, I'm thinking again about AR and have been playing around with a couple of less demanding social media app concepts. Our son came up with a clever way for people to connect called *Smoke Break*. The idea is simple: type your name or a nickname into the app and select a picture from the camera roll to identify yourself. When you hold the phone flat in your hand it shows where you and others who are using the app are located on a map. If you raise the phone and look through an AR viewer it shows others around you within about a city block. Names and pictures remain visible as long as the app is running. When you close the app, pictures are replaced with a puff of smoke to indicate someone was there.

Figure 19 Screenshots from *EZ Tide* (left) and *Geo Data* (right).

Summer 2011

One day at the beach as we wondered if the tide was coming in or going out, my brother-in-law said I should develop a tide app. Even though there are several out there I decided to make my own tide app. This is the freedom I have as an independent developer. What for-profit company would decide to do something that has already been done? Even more to the point, what company would be selling the crazy collection of apps that I have turned out over the past few years? Not many.

Although the general pattern of tides is governed by the moon, tide times vary locally. My new app called *EZ Tide* sends your GPS location to a PHP program running on a server that finds the nearest NOAA (National Oceanographic and Atmospheric Administration) tide station, retrieves its web page, parses the page for tide times, and sends the data back to the app. Getting the hang of PHP, I created another app called *GeoData* that displays global change data layers in a map viewer. Layers include land use/land cover derived from AVHRR satellite imagery, elevation, population density, and sea level rise. Perhaps the most unique feature of the app is the ability to display the extent of predicted rises in sea level that would result from the melting of the West Antarctic and Greenland ice sheets.

I've done a lot of academic research over the years in change detection and so it was only a matter of time before I made a change detection app, or two. One is a video CD app I call *Far Out Flicks*[19] that does real-time video processing and compositing. Instead of requiring a "green screen" to isolate objects, *Far Out Flicks* uses CD to cut and paste moving objects from video into image backgrounds. It can also produce some weird psychedelic effects, hence the name. My other CD app called *Mo'Talk* generates synthetic speech utterances whenever something moves in the camera view. The app uses an open-source text-to-speech synthesis program developed by Alan Black at CMU called *Festival-Lite* or *Flite* for short. I developed *MoTalk* as a stand-in for someone (like myself) who sometimes has to sit at a booth at a trade show and say the same thing over and over again. It is also a great gag app.

Fall 2011

Over the past three years, I have accumulated a lot of cool technology components and am starting to formulate app concepts that combine them in unusual ways. The name of my latest app, *Mapster = Maps + Multimedia,* says it all. After all, why stop at pictures and video – why not add sound files and other media to maps? With *Mapster*, you can (take a deep breath) add photo-overlays, floating images and icons, panoramic photographs, and sound files (songs) to maps, choose between map and augmented/virtual reality viewers, view metadata with embedded text, pictures, video, and audio files, use the *Flite* speech synthesizer to tell you the range and heading to a selected map object or read its metadata, import/export maps and media to/from your computer, email, or network links, capture maps/overlays with screenshots to use when there is no internet service, view dynamic data downloaded from network links, measure distances and areas on maps, search for places using a built-in gazetteer, and more.

---

[19] https://youtu.be/8bjrd6Ml8_8

I think I finally hit the wall. This method of development is crazy. Combining so many components in this way is leading to apps that are hard to maintain and even harder to describe in simple terms what they actually do.

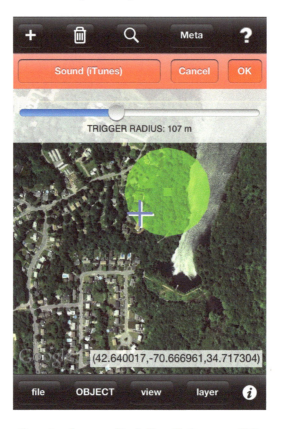

Figure 20 *Mapster* allowed you to place any kind of media in space. This example is a sound file that automatically plays when you approach its virtual location.

Modus Operandi

> This is the real secret of life – to be completely engaged with what you are doing in the here and now. And instead of calling it work, realize it is play. – Alan Watts.

At the beginning of my fourth year as an app developer, I have over fifty apps listed on iTunes and have sold over 30,000 units. A pattern of serial development – my *modus operandi* – continues. I have released two more spinoffs of the AR code I wrote a couple of years ago. *There You Are!* is a simple AR viewer that shows where others who are using the app are located. All you have to do to find someone using the app is to hold up your phone and look around. *Virtual Billboard* is a concept app for replacing the visual pollution of physical billboards. With it, you can create an ad or message that appears in an AR view as a graphic floating at a particular location in space. People are using *Virtual Billboard* to sell stuff, and post messages.

Figure 21 *Virtual Billboard* is a free app that lets you advertise your stuff to anyone who has it.

Winter 2012

Years ago, when people asked what I did for a living, I told them I developed algorithms. If that didn't kill the conversation, it certainly altered its course. Now, when I tell people that I develop apps, I kind of feel like a rock star. They say, "Cool. I have this great idea for an app," and go on to tell me that I should do it. A lot of really good ideas are beyond my skill set, involving social media, databases, merchandising, e-commerce, etc.

My sister-in-law, who is a photographer, suggested something I could do – a kind of game app that tests visual skills by finding differences between photos. The app called *Photo Eye Q* contains 50 photo puzzles, which she created from her photographs. Some differences are obvious, others are more subtle. The app evaluates your performance and posts your score online.

With all its cool sensors, I have three new iPhone sensor apps. The first is a heartbeat monitor that measures your heart rate using the iPhone's accelerometer. If you place your forearm on the edge of a table and look closely, you'll see that it shakes. On closer inspection, there is a subtle motion caused by your heartbeat. The app uses the accelerometer to sense the movement of your hand and then finds your pulse by feeding the signal from the accelerometer into a filter bank that looks for a periodic signal. Although *Heart Rate Display* can be quite accurate, the app description makes it clear that it should not be used for critical medical applications. Some users have told me that the app doesn't work because its theory of operation is not based on established methods, but it really does work, if it is used according to the directions.

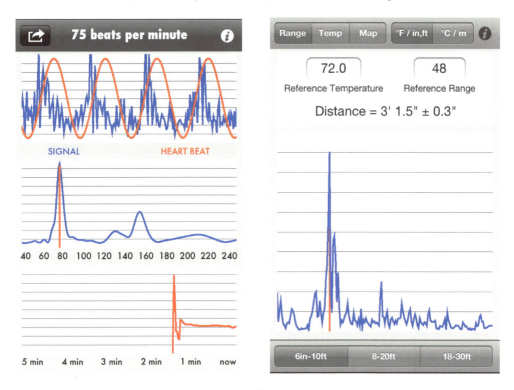

Figure 22 *Heart Rate Display*[20] (left) and *Sonic Utility* (right).

---

[20] https://youtu.be/nnBgwdXHwRs

The second sensor app uses sound to measure distance. *Sonic Utility* sends out a special kind of sound called a "chirp" from the iPhone's bottom speaker. The sound, reflected by nearby surfaces, is picked up by the microphone next to the speaker a short time later. A signal processing algorithm correlates the transmitted and received chirps, the latter of which is delayed in time by an amount t equal to twice the distance to the reflecting surface d divided by the speed of sound c. Knowing the speed of sound gives the distance as a function of time $2d=ct$. Although there are other apps that use sound to measure distance, *Sonic Utility* is the only one that can tell you the temperature. Since the speed of sound depends on temperature, if you know the distance to a reflecting surface, you can use the app to estimate the temperature. A third option uses the iPhone's gyro to generate a "sonic map" of your surroundings as you spin around in a circle.

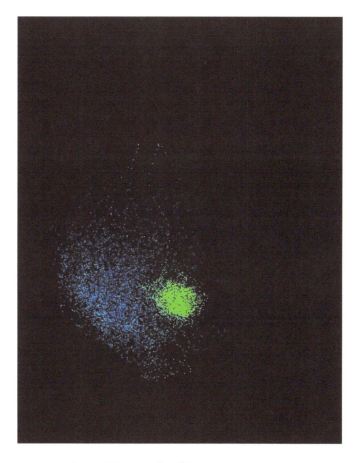

Figure 23 Screenshot from *Magneto-Vision*.

The third sensor app, *Magneto-Vision,* is another app that exploits the magnetometer. Unlike my earlier *MAD* app which simply detects differences in magnetic field strength, *Magneto-Vision* plots the direction of the change. One cool demonstration is to launch the app, turn on a nearby microwave oven, and watch what happens. I received an email the other day from a teacher who has used some of these apps to teach basic physics in school.

Spring 2012

Friends and family are surprised when I tell them I'm into local history. It was not my best subject in school. I've never been good at remembering names and dates. Plus, history seemed so cut and dry. For me, technology has turned out to be a great way to get out and experience history – and the experience has been far from cut and dry. Ironically, the failure of technology, namely a friend's buggy GPS receiver, got me into hiking and mapping in the first place. When I started mapping the Cape Ann woods in 2004, I used a handheld GPS, a digital camera, and a notebook. Now, as a result of the apps I have developed, all I need is an iPhone. It's like I'm Mr. Spock walking around with a *tricorder* in an episode of *Star Trek*. Over the past few years, I've collected hundreds of annotated geo-referenced photos with *iAtlas* and have used *KML Map* to rediscover long-lost and forgotten features in the woods. These apps have helped me construct a "spatial history" of the island woods of Cape Ann[21] – from colonial times to the present – something I never would have imagined (let alone cared about) as a kid.

Summer 2012

There is an ebb and flow to app development. As spring turns to summer, I'm more interested in working in the garden and going to the beach than writing code. One day at the beach, I'm reading a paper about FM synthesis and learn that it is possible to generate complex sounds using just one oscillator with feedback. So getting back to work, I'm thinking about a new kind of FM synth based on the same three oscillators I had already developed but connected in a completely different way. Instead of a fixed routing – oscillator 1 into oscillator 2 into oscillator 3 – why not connect them by means of a 3x3 routing matrix so that any oscillator can be connected to any other oscillator(s) creating all kinds of feedback opportunities? My new cross-modulated synthesizer, which I call *xMod*, has a much-improved reverb unit, a touch-sensitive keyboard, and a built-in MIDI player.[22] The app has 32 preset sounds from the conventional to the bizarre. *xMod* is unique and a distinct group of users like it; however, the retro look of the synth does not pass muster with the *trendinistas* – one reviewer said it looked like something made in the 90s. Hey, for someone who grew up in the 1960s, that was good enough for me.

---

[21] Mark Carlotto, *The Island Woods*, Create Space Independent Publishers, 2012, 2017.
[22] https://www.youtube.com/watch?v=xdQ6hGsiviw

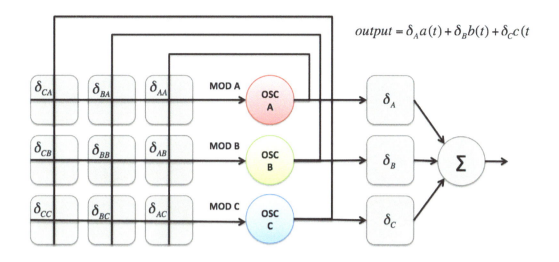

$$output = \delta_A a(t) + \delta_B b(t) + \delta_C c(t)$$

$$a(t) = A\sin\left(2\pi f_A t + \delta_{AA} a(t) + \delta_{BA} b(t) + \delta_{CA} c(t)\right)$$

$$b(t) = B\sin\left(2\pi f_A R_{BA} t + \delta_{BA} a(t) + \delta_{BB} b(t) + \delta_{CB} c(t)\right)$$

$$c(t) = C\sin\left(2\pi f_A R_{CA} t + \delta_{CA} a(t) + \delta_{CB} b(t) + \delta_{CC} c(t)\right)$$

Figure 24 *xMod* three-oscillators per key with feedback design (top) and app screenshot (bottom).

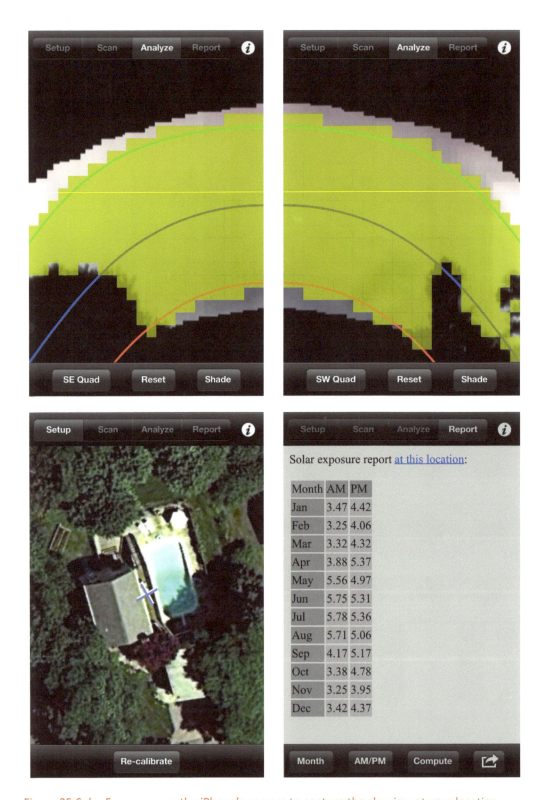

Figure 25 *Solar Exposure* uses the iPhone's camera to capture the sky view at your location (bottom left). The user marks open areas (top). The app computes the number of hours of direct sunlight (clouds excluded) per month (bottom right).

Fall 2012

I ended up having trouble this past summer with my tomato plants. The weather was warm, but the tomatoes didn't do well. I'm thinking that they're not getting enough sunlight, but it's hard to know for sure. So, I decided to develop an app that measures the amount of sunlight at a given location. *Solar Exposure* has an AR viewer that displays the seasonal path of the sun in the iPhone's camera view. You start by spinning around in a circle to record a 360° scan of your surroundings. Next, you mark obstructions such as buildings, trees, and other objects that block the sun in the scanned image. The app combines the obscuration map with the path of the sun to tell you when and for how long the sun is visible each day at your location.

I've also been experimenting with a new key detection algorithm based on what I call a "circular" voting scheme. In music theory, the "circle of fifths" depicts the progression of musical keys from C major to G major to D major, etc., all the way around to F major and back to C major. My new app called *KeyOmeter* combines the circle of major keys with that of their relative minor keys – A minor to E minor, B minor, and so on. Nearby keys such as the dominant, sub-dominant, and relative minor are next to the tonic making the display much easier to read. Instead of a bar graph jumping up and down from key to key, the circular display changes smoothly in a more intuitive way as a song modulates from one key to the next.

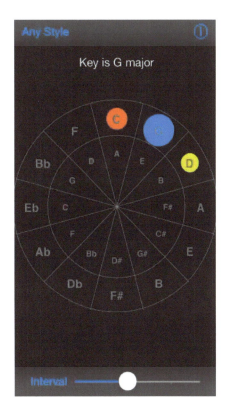

Figure 26 *KeyOmeter* displays the musical key of a song on the "circle of fifths" in real time.

I have removed a number of apps from iTunes for various reasons. Some were not well thought out, others didn't work, and a few never sold. *MUSYS* was originally designed as a tool to help understand music by displaying, notes, chords, keys, etc. A lot of people who bought *MUSYS* didn't know what to do with it. Rather than scrapping an app altogether, another option is to pivot – to change direction and redesign it. So I turned *MUSYS* into a new fun kind of app that helps one to understand music by playing along – I call the concept "analysis through synthesis." It works for any song in your iTunes library. As a song plays, pitch, chord, and key detection algorithms figure out melodic fragments, chords, and scales. Different play modes let you play along with the melody, add accompanying chords, and do scale-based improvisation.

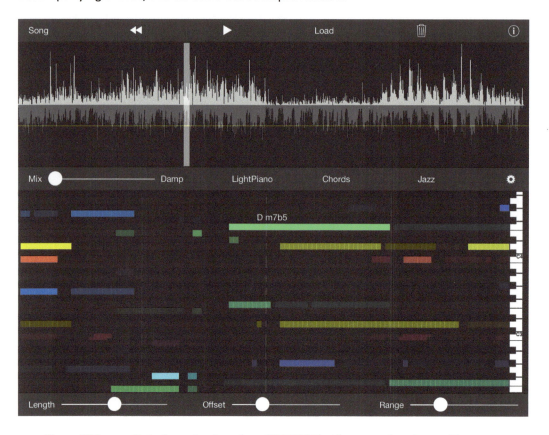

Figure 27 Screenshot of a revised version of *MUSYS* that lets you play along with a song.

Customer Service

The resistance to the unpleasant situation is the root of suffering. - Ram Dass

Sales have leveled off at about 10,000 apps per year. Last year, I added a dozen new apps, removed a few old ones, and started spending more time fixing bugs and adding new features to existing apps. With more than three-dozen apps currently listed on iTunes, I am spending less time on development and more time on customer service.

One day, while checking out the competition on the app store, I find a music app with hundreds of reviews – all 5-star. Not even a popular app like *Garage Band* is 5-star. So I learn that there's this thing called a "click farm" – a bunch of people who get paid to use and post reviews about apps. For a while, I thought this is how you played the game and looked into it. I have to admit, I did think about buying clicks. But then, when I was about to do it, I changed my mind. It wasn't right. It didn't matter if I sold a lot of apps or had a lot of good reviews. I had to play fair; otherwise, it meant nothing.

Winter 2013

All I've had time for is a few spinoffs. In January, I released a free AR app called *Floating Fotos* that lets you take a picture and post it in space for you and others who own the app to see. Next came *xMod Lite,* a stripped-down version of *xMod* that uses just a graphical interface (no control knobs) to change the timbre of the sound. The interface is a 2D visual representation of the synth's control settings (e.g., attack, release, modulation index, etc.). Each unique combination of control settings can be thought of as a point in an underlying 15-dimensional control "space." I call the visual representation a "sound space" as points close to one another correspond to similar synth settings and hence similar sounds. Timbres can be selected and mixed by tapping and dragging icons

Figure 28 *Floating* Fotos AR app.

around the screen. *Bach Machine*[23] is *xMod Lite* with a button that randomly selects and plays one of several hundred Bach sonatas, concertos, etc., which I scraped from the internet. *Bach Machine* is my tribute to the 1968 album, *Switched on Bach* by Walter Carlos. Like the original Moog synthesizer keyboard controller, the app has a "wood finish" to give it a baroque look.

Figure 29 Bach Machine used a "sound space" to change timbre.

Spring 2013

A lot of musicians use apps to look up chords, play chord progressions, etc. Some take a song and generate a sequence of chords. I decided to repackage the chord detection algorithms used in *Pitch to Note +* and *MUSYS* in a real-time app called *What Chord* that displays chord notes on a piano keyboard along with the name of the chord. A variation of this app called *Auto Chord* converts chords into MIDI notes and sends them to a networked synth. As with my first combination pitch detector/synth app, *Sound from Sound Synth*, *Auto Chord* still has latency issues. However, using it with discretion (and headphones to prevent feedback), *Auto Chord* generates a great "string wash" to accompany solo piano or guitar.[24]

Summer 2013

Most synths generate sound using oscillators, filters, envelope generators, modulators, and mixers. But there are other methods. With the advent of radio in the 1920s, artists

---

[23] https://www.youtube.com/watch?v=gw9qhJLXNFo&pbjreload=10
[24] https://www.youtube.com/watch?v=yZaDbSnmXV4

began to invent ways of making music in all sorts of unconventional ways. Capturing and manipulating sound with tape machines was the most popular method. One of my favorites from this genre known as *musique concrète*[25] is a 1968 composition for six shortwave radios by Karlheinz Stockhausen. The Mellotron, an instrument popularized by groups like the Moody Blues and King Crimson, was the first sampled sound instrument that stored pre-recorded sounds on tape loops. Digital samplers use the sample principle with the tape loop replaced with a chunk of memory. Either way, the samples have to be extracted by some means, usually manually, from live audio or recordings. My latest app *Auto Sampler* uses the pitch detector in *Pitch to Note* to automatically detect and capture sound samples. An especially useful feature of the app is that it automatically determines the musical pitch of the extracted samples.

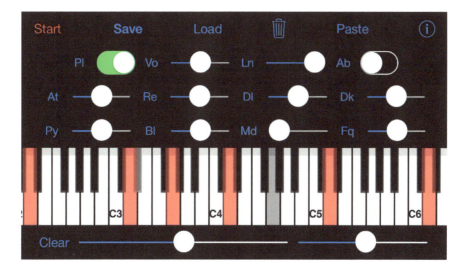

Figure 30 *Auto Sampler* app.

Toward the end of summer, I released an enhanced version of *xMod* called *Uber Synth*. With the power of iOS devices steadily increasing it was time to add another layer or voice to the synth. In *Uber Synth,* two different timbres (e.g., flute and cello) can be assigned to each note. I also came up with a couple of ways of changing the timbre dynamically. One way assigns different sounds to each part of the keyboard, which is programmed by pressing a key and tapping a sound icon in the sound space. As you play the instrument, sounds are blended spatially across the keyboard turning the synth into a weird kind of symphony orchestra. Another way involves selecting a region in the sound space within which the timbre automatically evolves each time you press a key or a programmable timer fires.

---

[25] https://en.wikipedia.org/wiki/Musique_concrète

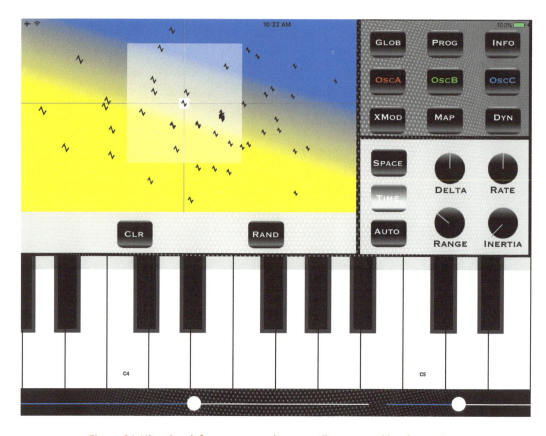

Figure 31 *Uber Synth* features two three-oscillator sound banks per key.

My apps are decidedly not mainstream. I don't try to be different. It's just the way it is. Being an app developer has taught me to accept both praise and criticism. Customer service is not what I signed up for in the beginning but is part of the responsibility of selling a product. Disgruntled users love to vent in iTunes reviews. Most, however, contact me directly via email with problems and feedback. I'm always happy to examine screenshots, images, files, and whatever else is necessary to diagnose and fix their problem and can usually get a new version of the app with a fix uploaded in a couple of days.

Fall 2013

I am fortunate to have been to Stonehenge and seen the pyramids in Egypt. Ancient mysteries are in other parts of the world, not where I live, right? A local poet by the name of Charles Olson saw Gloucester as a microcosm of the world – that everything that happened out there could be found here. So, it came as no small surprise to have just met a local anthropologist who believes a place in Gloucester called Poles Hill might have been the site of an ancient Native American solar observatory – a solar calendar not unlike Stonehenge.

Starting with a couple of photographs, I located a strange-looking boulder near the center of the site that serves as a viewing location" and a large boulder to the northwest called the "sunset rock" and have determined that a summer solstice sunset alignment does indeed exist between them. Hundreds of glacial erratics – boulders transported by glaciers of the last Ice Age – dot this beautiful but desolate landscape. Wondering whether other alignments existed, I identified a number of candidates using Google Earth imagery and uploaded their geo-coordinates to *KML Map*. Using the app to navigate along rabbit trails and through brush I eventually located and photographed two unusual rock formations. One, at the winter solstice sunrise location, turned out to be two stacked granite slabs. The other, located in the summer solstice sunrise direction, looked a lot like the sunset rock.

The investigation expanded. Local archaeologists came and reviewed our work. Drones collected HD video over the site. Meanwhile, I developed an app that turns the iPhone into a remote-sensing device for collecting overhead imagery.[26] The key component in *Aerial Camera* is what's called a camera model – a set of mathematical equations that map image pixel coordinates in the camera view to latitude and longitude coordinates on the ground. The app projects the camera view in real-time to a map using the latitude, longitude, and elevation of the device supplied by the iPhone's GPS, the azimuth angle, provided by the magnetometer, and the tilt, yaw, and roll angles measured by the inertial measurement unit. The iPhone's IMU is what counts steps in fitness apps, and is a critical component in gaming and AR.

Attached to a selfie stick that I made from a pole I use to clean my swimming pool, I am using *Aerial Camera* to collect high-resolution KML image overlays of the stone features on Poles Hill. Given the limited accuracy of the iPhone's sensors, the imagery doesn't line up exactly with the ground, but is close and can be adjusted in Google Earth. Perhaps it is my imagination but certain stones at the site appear to have a serpent-like shape, especially when viewed from above – not something I expected to find on a rocky hilltop in my hometown.

---

[26] Mark J. Carlotto, "Fusing Maps with Photos from Mobile Devices", *SPIE Defense and Security*, 5-8 May 2014, Baltimore, MD (Paper 9091-41).

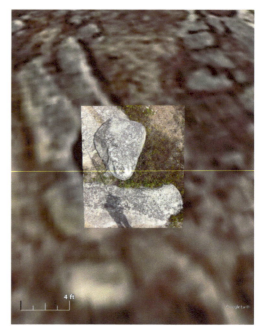

Figure 32 Author with iPhone mounted to the end of a pole (left) running *Aerial Camera* app used to image rock formations atop Poles Hill. Zoomed in on an area of interest with a photo from *Aerial Camera* registered to Google Earth (right).

The Pain of Progress

> I know engineers, they love to change things. –
> Dr. McCoy, *Star Trek*[27]

I haven't developed or updated an app in months and I'm having a hard time getting back into it. It seems a number of apps no longer work. Each time Apple releases a new version of the operating system, some piece of code that used to do this or that doesn't work anymore, or worse, crashes.

Winter 2014

In the process of updating and getting older apps to work once again, I've developed

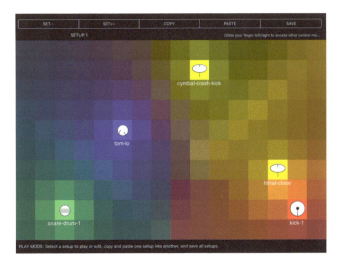

Figure 33 *Drum Space* app.

three new apps. The first is called *Drum Space*. Many drum apps let you build your own set by placing a drum here, a cymbal there, etc. *Drum Space* exploits the space in between drums by creating a continuous palette of sound. Tapping anywhere on the screen blends nearby samples. As you tap left to right, sounds move left to right in space. Tapping from top to bottom goes from sounds that are softer, have more reverb, and seem farther away, to sounds that are louder, have less reverb, and seem closer to you.

The second new app *Oasis* extracts pitched samples from songs. Originally, *Auto Sampler* had this capability. In the process of updating the app, I removed it because the user didn't have any control over where in the song the samples were taken. *Oasis* gives you that control. The user interacts with a waveform display of the sound. Any part of the song can be accessed by sliding your finger to that part of the waveform. Extracted samples can be played on the app or exported to *Auto Sampler* using iOS pasteboard cut and paste.

My third new app, *Orbulator,* resulted from a recent update of *Mandala Music.*

---

[27] https://youtu.be/7OzbKckkaJU?si=EKa9y2d2GaxjQKUp

Orbulator consists of eight touch-sensitive "orbs" (pads) surrounding a larger central orb. Like *Mandala Music,* the orbs are mapped into one of 33 user-selectable musical scales – from Western major and minor to Eastern and Middle Eastern modal. With an enhanced two-oscillator FM synth, *Orbulator* has four voices per orb capable of some pretty bizarre sounds with names such as "High Voltage," "Mogwai," "Dolphin," "Wet One," "Elastic Band," "Odd Bright" and others. *xMod* and *Uber Synth* have gesture recognizers for pitch bending and tremolo – sliding your finger left-right on the keyboard changes pitch ± 1 semitone and sliding up-down varies the volume. In *Orbulator*, finger movement within an orb can be programmed to vary pitch, volume, and modulation. To make the app easier to use out of the box I added a "roll of the dice" button that randomly selects sound settings and scales, and an autoplay feature that generates weird pseudo-random music.[28] These new apps, especially *Orbulator*, are definitely not mainstream, but those who like them, like them.

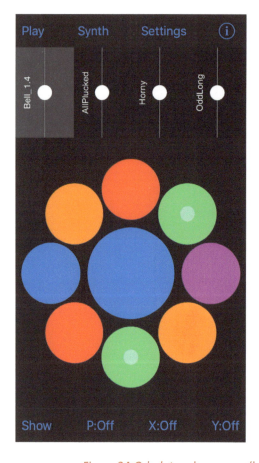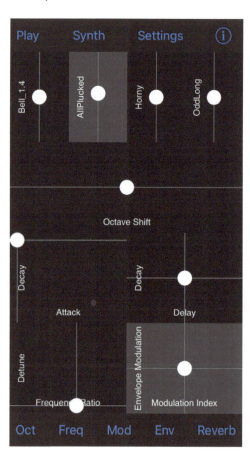

Figure 34 *Orbulator* play screen (left) and synthesizer controls (right).

_____

[28] https://www.youtube.com/watch?v=7J6YeerW1h4

Spring 2014

As spring breaks I'm back at Poles Hill and have created still another app, this one to deal with a problem at the site that I've been trying to understand for a few months. The summer solstice alignment has a clear line of sight between the central viewing location and the sunset rock, but the other two alignments I discovered do not. The problem is that the other sight lines are obscured by trees and brush. I need a way to correlate sight lines on Google Earth with ground photography to verify 1) whether a clear line of sight does in fact exist, and 2) if so, what trees and bushes need to be trimmed/removed to see these sighting stones from the gnomon. Although there are several panoramic photo apps for sale on iTunes that capture wide-angle views they cannot be tied to external geo-data. My new *Gyro Scan* app uses the iPhone's magnetometer and gyro to generate a 360° view that can be exported as a KML photo overlay and viewed on Google Earth. After trimming and removing a few trees and some bushes with the help of *Gyro Scan* we can now see all three solstice markers from the center of the site.

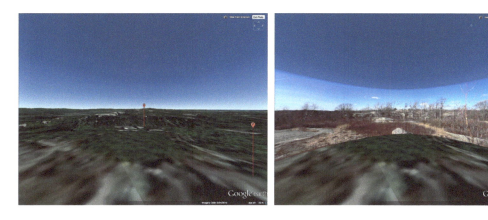

Figure 35 Google Earth ground view (left) with *Gyro Scan* 360° photo overlay (right).

Summer 2014

The more I play around with the *Flite* speech synth the more I like it. It is a nice piece of code. I decided to make a text-to-speech app that you can play like a musical instrument. I call it *Tap Rap*. Sounds are programmed and played using a 4x4 array of touch pads. Each pad is programmed independently by typing in one or more words or phonetic fragments, selecting a voice (male or female), musical pitch, rate, and variation. Although *Tap Rap* is not a music app *per se* it can be programmed to do a decent rendering of "Mr. Roboto" or sing "Happy Birthday" in a robot voice that you can text or email to your friends.

As summer comes to a close, I released a couple of utility apps. *MetaPict* shows the location and direction a photo was taken on a map view. It also displays EXIF metadata about when the picture was taken, its exposure, and other information. *Readerz* turns your iPhone into a pair of reading glasses. When my eyesight began to change a few years ago, I noticed that while my ability to see in normal light decreased, I could still see well enough to read a newspaper in bright sunlight. *Readerz* uses video image enhancement to increase contrast in low-light situations, like at a fancy restaurant. It can help those who forget their reading glasses to read a menu, concert program, or newspaper article with their iPhone.

Figure 36 Readerz app contrast enhancement (left) and magnifying glass (right).

Fall 2014

I face a growing list of apps that no longer work. It seems that as the pace of technological progress quickens, the "pain of progress" increases. We all know about "planned obsolescence" – the business model that forces you to buy a new iPhone every couple of years. New phones and new features require more frequent operating system updates, which drive an increased frequency of app updates, some happening every week or so. As the complexity of the underlying software increases with expanded frameworks and new ways of doing things, app developers must spend more and more time keeping apps in working order.

So for a developer, the pleasure of creating a new app inevitably leads to the pain of having to update it. Checking sales, I've sold about 60,000 units thus far and developed more than 80 apps with about 50 currently listed in iTunes. That's a lot of future updates. I should probably reduce the number of apps to a more manageable number and/or stop making new ones. Unfortunately, I can do neither. Plotting rank-ordered sales reveal an exponential distribution with no clear-cut threshold differentiating good and bad apps in terms of sales. Besides, some of my worst-selling apps such as *Orbulator* are my favorites.

From the instant gratification of my first year as an app developer to the pain of progress in my sixth year, I begin to wonder if it is time to quit and move on to some other pursuit.

A New Direction

> Muddy water is best cleared by leaving it alone.
> – Alan Watts

I haven't released a new app in months. There's no time. I'm spending all my free time doing updates. A third-party inter-app audio framework known as Audiobus was introduced in 2013. Inter-app audio allows apps that produce, modify, record, and analyze audio data to communicate with one another. More and more users are asking for Audiobus so I have decided to add it to a number of my apps.

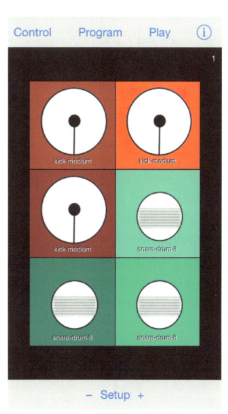

Figure 37 Screenshots from *MIDI TTS* (left) and *Wrist Rhythm* (right).

Winter 2015

Following a similar pattern as last winter, some recent app updates have led to a couple of new apps. *MIDI TTS* is a MIDI-controlled version of the *Flite* text-to-speech synthesizer that I used in *Tap Rap*. The app has 128 MIDI programmable pads that generate pitched speech sounds when triggered. The app has turned out to be unexpectedly weird, but fun.[29] The other app is a new kind of MIDI drum controller

---

[29] https://www.youtube.com/watch?v=6x3TBvfQrYg

called *Wrist Rhythm*. I recently updated *World Drums* to be MIDI-controllable and thought why not use gesture recognizers instead of pads to trigger drum sounds. Holding the iPhone in your hand, six basic wrist gestures can be detected with its IMU: rotate clockwise or counterclockwise, tilt up or down, and yaw left or right. *Wrist Rhythm* assigns these gestures to MIDI notes. When a gesture is detected *Wrist Rhythm* can send a MIDI note to a drum synth, or play a sample on the app. For example, a performer could program and play *Wrist Rhythm* as a tambourine. Although the app works pretty well, it does not seem to be catching on as a MIDI controller. I guess a tambourine is a lot cheaper than an iPhone.

Spring 2015

My dad passed away in April. He was a radio operator during World War II and later became an electrical engineer. If it wasn't for my dad's advice, I might be the drummer in the band playing tonight at the bar down the street, which would have been good, instead of doing what I'm doing, which is better. Thanks, Dad.

A paper on our work at Poles Hill was published in the spring issue of the *Bulletin of the Massachusetts Archaeological Society*.[30] In the meantime, I completed a new book on Dogtown called *The Cellars Speak*[31] that combines mapping and genealogical research to determine who lived where and when in Dogtown – a project I have been working on, off and on, for more than ten years. As the weather turns warmer, I'm spending more time in the woods and less time in front of a computer screen.

Figure 38 Photo of my dad in the late 1930s appearing to hold an early version of the iPhone.

Summer 2015

One day a friend of mine joked that I live in a place surrounded by water, yet I spend most of my time in the woods. "You should do something related to the ocean," he said. Not knowing what to do next, this summer, I started a new project that involves just that – putting an iPhone into a watertight container and lowering it into the ocean to

---

[30] Mary Ellen Lepionka and Mark J. Carlotto, "Evidence of a Native American Solar Observatory on Sunset Hill in Gloucester, Massachusetts," *Bulletin of the Massachusetts Archaeological Society*, Vol. 76, No. 1, Spring 2015.

[31] Mark Carlotto, *The Cellars Speak*, Create Space Independent Publishers, 2015.

collect underwater imagery for hours at a time. The device, which I call an *AquiPod,* uses the iPhone as an underwater sensor. It all started when some friends decided to build a "driftBot" using a Raspberry Pi computer with an added camera and various sensors to collect scientific data and imagery. The original vision was quite ambitious – a device that could cross the ocean and send back data via satellite phone. By mid-summer, it appeared that the drifter would probably not be deployed this year and so I began to experiment with sometime simpler.

Figure 39 An *AquiPod* is an iPhone inside a watertight container plus an anchor that is deployed and operates at a fixed location underwater.

Figure 40 Author deploying *AquiPod* at Whale Cove in Rockport, Massachusetts.

I've been deploying *AquiPod* devices anchored at fixed locations to take long-duration time-lapse videos of crabs, lobsters, snails, skates, stripers, and other sea life. The videos are fascinating to watch and helpful in understanding and appreciating the ocean around us. Collecting good quality video an hour or more in length is not possible with the iPhone. Although there are time-lapse apps out there, I created a special app called *Extended Time* Lapse that is designed in such a way as to minimize power consumption so it can run all day. The app captures and stores each picture as a JPEG file so that if the app fails or the device runs out of power, any data already captured can still be read.

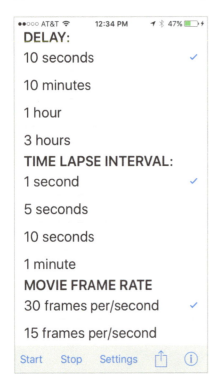 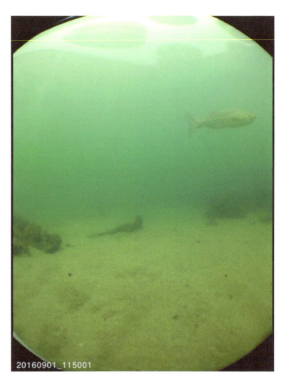

Figure 41 Control settings for *Extended Time Lapse* app (left) and a frame from a time-lapse video collected with an *AquiPod* (right).

Fall 2015

As I spend more time in the water and less time developing apps, the pain of progress has turned into the joy of discovery. As the weather turns cooler, I am starting to design new apps and underwater devices, which I hope to deploy next summer.

Back to the Future

Look deep into nature, and then you will
understand everything better. — Albert Einstein

Spending more time outdoors I have been updating my 3D photo and video apps and have come up with a new app called *Pan 3D* for taking 3D panoramic photographs. Like so many of my other apps, *Pan 3D* is built on the foundation of an earlier app. That app, *Gyro Scan*, creates a 360° photograph as you spin in a circle by assembling vertical scans into an image, in much the same way a photocopier scans a document. The easiest way to capture 3D is with two cameras side by side. There are dual-lens cameras out there, but they are not made by Apple. With only one lens, iPhone camera apps generate 3D by combing two views captured at different times. Although it is not possible to generate 3D with just rotation, it turns out that the *Gyro Scan* concept can be modified to extract two scans at the proper separation to produce a 360° wide 3D image. *Pan 3D* lets you generate and view your own 3D pan images, as well as images in standard 3D format downloaded from the web, with or without AR glasses.

Winter 2016

I attached a hydrophone to one of my new *AquiPod* devices to record underwater sounds. In the same way multiple microphones create an acoustic space, the thought occurred to me that it might be possible to create a similar space underwater by using hydrophones on two or more *AquiPods* deployed at different locations. Unlike wired microphones/hydrophones, however, there is a problem – that of synchronizing acoustic recordings between devices. If the synchronization problem can be solved it might be possible to track sounds that are moving in or under the water using iPhones.

Synchronization requires a common time reference. Although we know that there is no such thing as absolute time, iOS provides something called *mach_absolute_time*, which is the time in nanoseconds since a device was last booted. Every iOS device has its own mach_absolute_time clock. So, the solution I came up with is to correlate the mach_absolute_time of each device with a short external sound event such as a hand clap. Once synchronized, my new app *Sound Sync'd Recorder* records audio that can be synchronized with audio from other synchronized devices. The method works well enough to track a moving object using at least three devices.

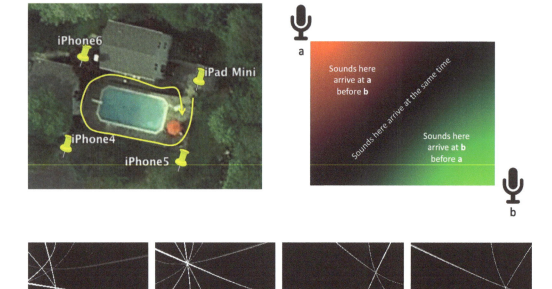

Figure 42 Detection of a moving object using acoustic data collected with four iOS devices (top left). A trilateration algorithm running on a Mac uses the speed of sound and delay of signals (determined by cross-correlation) to determine the object's distance from each iOS device (top right). Sample frames from the algorithm (bottom) follow a moving object around the swimming pool. Lines are cross-correlations between pairs of iOS devices. Intersections of the brightest lines (strongest cross-correlations) are possible object locations.

Spring 2016

The *AquiPod* operates at a fixed location. I am working on a new contraption that mounts an iPhone inside a smaller waterproof case so that it lies flat on the water's surface at the end of a boogie board. The top of the case is above water so the iPhone has GPS service. The camera is on the other side looking down. I modified *Extended Time Lapse* to geo-tag each picture that it takes. The idea is to float around with the boogie board as the camera photographically maps the bottom using GPS to mark the location of each photo. This new concept should work as long as the top of the case is out of the water.

Unfortunately, time-lapse photography is not particularly useful with a moving camera. But I have learned that video data can be attributed with geolocation just like a photograph. I have created a new app *Trek* Video by adding the ISO 6709 location metadata framework to some video recorder code. As you play a movie recorded with *Trek Video* the app plots the location of the camera as it moves on a map.

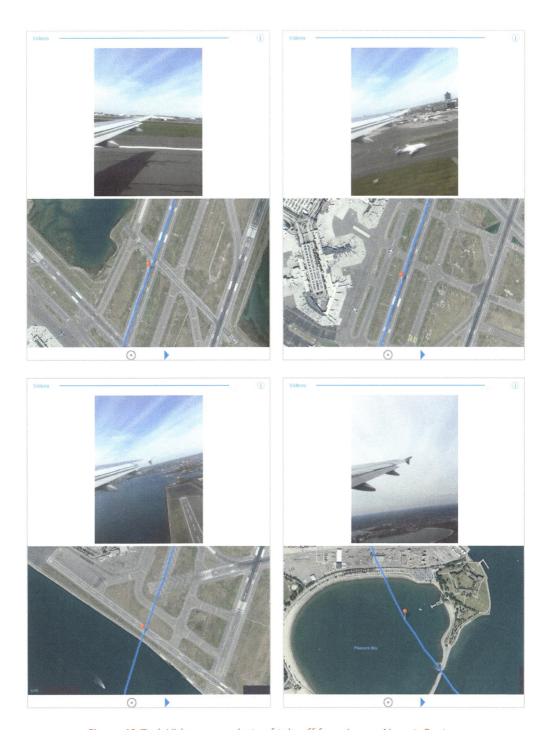

Figure 43 *Trek Video* screenshots of takeoff from Logan Airport, Boston.

Summer 2016

I tried with only marginal success at getting my new aquatic mapping device to work. On some days the water was not clear enough to see the bottom. On other days the surf was too rough to keep the top of the phone out of the water long enough for the GPS to work. The greatest success this summer was with the original moored *AquiPod*. An intern from a local college deployed the device at various locations around Cape Ann as part of a summer research project and captured some great time-lapse videos. As a result of our success, I was asked to put together four devices with iPhones and apps for a local maritime museum to collect underwater imagery of different marine habitats around Cape Ann for an exhibit they are planning for next year.

Fall 2016

The advantage of time-lapse is that it doesn't generate a lot of data. The disadvantage is that it's easy to miss something such as a fast-moving fish swimming past the camera. This got me thinking about a way of combining full-motion and time-lapse video using image change detection to vary the frame rate. When there isn't much action, the frame rate is low. When something changes, either entering, leaving, or moving around in the field of view, the change detector increases the frame rate. I call my new app *Elastic Video*. The amount of video compression depends on the amount of movement in the scene and is typically about 10:1. Elastic videos have a snap-action quality that are fun to watch.[32]

Figure 44 Frame from *Elastic Video* app capturing a squirrel (lower left) in my parent's backyard.

Meanwhile, *KML Map* and *KML Map HD* users are requesting dynamic network links, map overlays, geodata import, and other features. It is gratifying that people are using my apps.

---

[32] https://www.youtube.com/watch?v=6-XIWoMjjHQ

Figure 45 Some user applications built using *KML Map HD.*

Winter 2017

Before moving to Gloucester and becoming interested in local history and archaeology, I had been involved in a two-decade-long investigation of possible archaeological ruins on Mars. I showed that one of the objects resembling an enormous primate face was not an optical illusion as claimed by NASA but maintained its facial appearance over a wide range of lighting and viewing angles.

This past summer a couple of old Mars buddies asked me to take a look at some strange objects first spotted on the moon by the Apollo astronauts in the 1960s that had been recently re-imaged by the unmanned Lunar Reconnaissance Orbiter. I was skeptical about lunar anomalies given all the wild claims on the internet by people finding UFOs, cities, towers, and other fantastic objects on the moon. To my surprise, the objects I was shown in the crater Paracelsus on the far side of the moon were quite unusual and so decided to investigate them further.

Although there were multiple images of the objects, all were taken from roughly the same look angle. This was basically the situation in the early days of the Mars investigation. Using a method known as shape from shading developed in the 1960s to make 3D maps of the moon from lunar orbiter photos – I computed a height map from one of the images and used it to render computer-generated image (CGI) views from other directions. Analysis of these synthetic views suggested that one of the structures might have an inner space, possibly a passageway leading into an adjacent hillside and perhaps underground.

As we completed our analysis of the objects in the fall and wrote a paper later published by the *Journal of Space* Exploration[33] I decided to make some of the tools I had developed available as an app. *SFSX,* my first Mac app, takes an image, computes a 3D elevation model, and uses the image and model to generate CGI images and movies that show objects in the image from all directions. Not the sort of app most people would buy, but a must-have for others like me searching for anomalous objects on the surfaces of the moon, Mars, and other places.

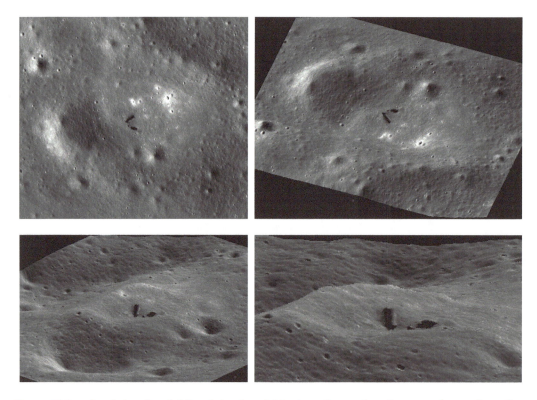

Figure 46 Overhead view (top left) and simulated CGI views from other directions (top right and bottom) based on a 3D model computed from the original image.

---

[33] Mark J. Carlotto, Francis L. Ridge, and Ananda L. Sirisena, "Image Analysis of Unusual Structures on the Far Side of the Moon in the Crater Paracelsus C," *Journal of Space Exploration*, Vol. 4, Issue 3, 2016.

Refactoring

> It takes awhile to create nothing. — Martin
> Fowler

Since my epiphany a few years ago that the level of customer service is proportional to the number of apps, I began to thin the ranks. During my peak years, I had as many as sixty apps for sale on iTunes. At the start of my ninth year as an app developer, I am down to about four-dozen apps. It has taken me a while to realize that every app doesn't have to be its own distinct project. For example, I had more than a dozen apps that used a pitch detector and each one had its version. So, I began to refactor code, to organize groups of similar apps into projects that shared common algorithms and software with multiple targets, one for each app in the group.

Figure 47 *Pitch to Note* and related apps refactored as a single Xcode project.

Spring 2017

It's been about two years since I touched a music app. There was a lot to do. The latest version of Audiobus just released now supports MIDI allowing you to make MIDI as well as audio connections between apps. I had been using Apple's Core MIDI framework to route MIDI signals from apps such as *Voice Controller* and *Audio to MIDI* to networked synths. Now, to keep things simple, I decided to convert all my MIDI apps to Audiobus 3. I didn't have to put everything in one app, like a MIDI player in a synth. Apps could be simpler and more modular.

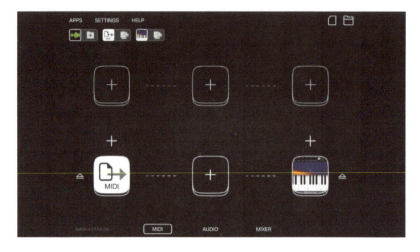

Figure 48 Using Audiobus to connect *MIDIplay* to *xMod*.

Summer 2017

For security reasons, iOS puts each app in a "sandbox" that limits access to files, preferences, network resources, hardware, etc. Apps have their own sandbox directory – a place in the file system for the app and its data. Apple's new iOS 11 operating system makes it easy to transfer data between apps, *iCloud*, and even *Dropbox* using their *Files* app. Developers often must "jump through hoops" to get things done in iOS. Audiobus 3 and iOS 11 are making it easier to connect and transfer data between apps. Morphing into a software engineer I am spending a lot of time modularizing apps, refactoring code, and redesigning UIs. *MIDIplay,* a new lightweight MIDI player app that I split off from *xMod*, is my only new iOS app this year.

Fall 2017

I've spent the last few months redesigning the *Audio to MIDI* app. The original concept was based on using real-time pitch detectors to extract musical notes from live audio. The pitch detector generated a lot of wrong notes, often from drums, cymbals, and other percussion instruments. When operating in real time there isn't a lot that can be done to "post-process" and remove the wrong notes before generating MIDI output, so I decide to redesign the app to run non-real time.

My initial thought was to use a machine learning approach to do a better job of converting audio to MIDI notes. However, a review of current research and available products suggests the best results are obtained by converting a single melodic line, or a particular instrument such as a piano, usually trained on a limited set of songs and musical styles. My long-term goal is to create an algorithm that will work with any kind of music with a minimum of wrong notes.

Figure 49 Screenshots from an updated version of *Audio to MIDI Recorder*

So rather than use machine learning, I have decided to exploit some basic concepts in psychoacoustics to improve performance. Where "seeing" occurs in space and time, "hearing" happens in time and frequency. 2D Gabor filter banks have been shown to be good models for what happens in the early stages of processing in the visual cortex. A similar kind of filter known as a gamma tone plays a similar role in the early stages of pitch perception. *Pitch to Note* used a simple recursive filter that tended to misfire on wide-band noise-like sounds such as drums and cymbals. The gamma tone filter turns out to be much less sensitive to these sounds so ends up producing fewer wrong notes.

Pitch is one dimension of musical perception. Rhythm is the other. Evidence suggests that the auditory system segments sound based on what are called onsets. If the app does not have to operate in real-time the audio data can be passed through the gamma tone filter bank to extract pitch data and through a difference of Gaussians filter to detect onsets. Combining the two we can obtain a more reliable pitch estimate. The redesigned *Audio to MIDI* app provides several options for fusing pitch and rhythm information depending on the characteristics of the music.[34] Although there is still plenty of room for improvement, the latest update goes well beyond the performance of previous versions and is a significant step forward. Long term, I have high hopes for this app.

---

[34] https://www.youtube.com/watch?v=Jk9nUbOr2iI

89.3K Units | Lifetime: April 2003 – August 2023 | UTC ˅

Content   Territory   Device   Category   Content Type   Transaction Type   CMB   Version   Client

Units per Month   Area ˅   Months ˅

	Name	Type	Platforms	Apple ID	Units
1	What Key Mark Carlotto	App	iOS	302005959	6.77K
2	Pitch To Note Mark Carlotto	App	iOS	293347132	3.77K
3	World Drums Mark Carlotto	App	iOS	331448543	3.70K
4	Audio to MIDI Mark Carlotto	App	iOS	320560554	3.65K
5	Tap Rap Mark Carlotto	App	iOS	815036364	3.24K
6	KML Map HD Mark Carlotto	App	iOS	386832667	3.21K
7	Floating Fotos Mark Carlotto	App	iOS	582703171	2.87K
8	Mandala Music Mark Carlotto	App	iOS	312681681	2.84K
9	KML Map Mark Carlotto	App	iOS	347857461	2.79K
10	"Smoke Break" Mark Carlotto	App	iOS	428940144	2.51K

Show More

Figure 50 Apple's App Connect site shows 90,000 units sold in 15 years. September 2017 was my peak month with more than 5500 units sold. By far, *What Key* and other music apps were the best sellers, followed by *KML Map* and *KML Map HD*.

Enlightenment through Development

> Creativity is allowing yourself to make mistakes.
> Art is knowing which ones to keep. – Scott
> Adams

In May 2008 my wife and I spent a week in Rome. The trip was paid for with the money I made in my first few months of app development. I had a half-dozen apps listed on iTunes and was selling about 30 units each day. Not enough to live on but enough to take a trip once in a while. My most popular apps were *Pitch to Note, What Key,* and *iAtlas.* They were cool but not apps that you had to have. I ignored emails that offered to increase sales through advertising and by offering various promotions and deals as it seemed unlikely they would increase sales enough to justify the expense. Instead, I decided to increase sales by making more apps. After all, I had a lot of ideas. I began to dream of a steadily increasing revenue stream fueled purely by ideas.

But then, something unexpected happened. It always does. Over time, I noticed that as I cranked out more apps, sales per app started to decrease. There weren't a lot of apps in 2008 and so there wasn't a lot of competition. Even a weird app like *Resonizer* sold. But the situation was changing. Apple no longer featured the newest apps up front on iTunes. With the number of apps growing exponentially, iTunes now put the best-selling ones at the top of the list. New apps were taking longer to be noticed, and more and more from listings on third-party sites.

As I awoke from my pipe dream, I realized that I was benefiting from app development in other less tangible ways. Besides the creative aspect, which has always been the most enjoyable part of the process, I was getting into making apps better. It turned out that the nature of the work I was doing in my day job also started to change. For years I had been tasked with coming up with novel algorithms and concepts, but we now had a new project that involved getting all the technology I had developed over the years to actually work. My boss put it this way, "We need to get all this stuff working for real, no shit."

So, day and night I was becoming more committed to making things work. This might sound strange but coming up with a new idea in R&D, whether it is an algorithm or an app, usually culminates in what's called "a proof of concept demonstration" – basically, showing that it works. But "working" is a relative term. When I was fresh out of school, getting an algorithm to work meant showing results on a small data set, a couple of images. Later, it became developing an algorithm on one set of data and testing it on another. Now it meant releasing a piece of software that had to work, no shit. And if it didn't, it had to be fixed. Spiral development had become a spiral of updates with many being fixes to unanticipated problems, problems thought to be pathological – occurring almost never, to occurring all of the time. These new experiences were like a baptism of data into a larger reality.

That reality was not just making something, it was making it better. Making apps better is not an end in itself but is a process that combines the science of app development – better algorithms that increase algorithm performance and reliability – with the art of app development – improving the user experience and the elegance of doing whatever it is the app does. The process of making an app better is driven to a large extent by customer feedback. When you put something out there you have to be able to accept praise and criticism equally well. Achieving that state of equipoise is as difficult in app development as it is in life. A big part of my enlightenment through development is having developed so many apps that I don't feel a strong connection to any one of them. As a result, I take criticism as "Hey, this doesn't work, fix it." There's nothing personal about it.

Still, I am interested in developing new apps and still have a lot of ideas. In ten years, I've accumulated a lot of cool technology components such as pitch detectors, FM synths, change detectors, camera models, augmented reality viewers, etc. I can think of so many more ways of putting these components together. For example, I have always been fascinated with cross-media applications that convert pictures and movement into music (sonification) and music into visualizations, maybe based on physics or musical principles instead of whatever Apple uses in their iTunes Visualizer, which is not a criticism by any means. I love watching the visualizer. (Perhaps it has something to do with growing up in the 1960s.) Another area I'd like to investigate is algorithms and apps that can learn musical styles from MIDI data and generate their own synthetic music that sounds like Bach or even Keith Emerson.

I put an iPhone in an *AquiPod*. Others have flown iPhones in balloons. Mobile devices are powerful computers with sensors and communications. What about putting an iPhone in a SmallSat? Crazy? Maybe.

One Foot In and One Foot Out

> Shit or get off the pot – Anonymous.

Switching gears once again, I published a book in the fall of 2018 on some new research concerning the possible existence of previous technological civilizations on Earth. In the summer of 2019, I released two new apps, *Sacred Directions*, and *Sacred Directions AR*. Like so many other apps I developed them because I needed something that didn't exist.

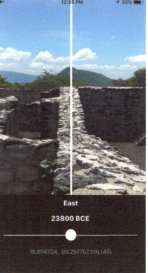

Figure 51 *Sacred Directions* is an archaeoastronomy app that plots astronomical alignments on Apple Map satellite images (top). *Sacred Directions AR* uses augmented reality to display astronomical alignments in the camera view of the iPhone (bottom right). The author using the app at Xochicalco, Mexico (bottom left).

I used them to analyze the alignments of hundreds of archaeological sites around the world. My theory was that about half of the sites that didn't seem to be aligned either astronomically (for example, to solstices or lunar standstills) or geographically (to true or magnetic north or to other sites) had been built over the ruins of earlier sites that were built when the North Pole was in a different location.[35] The idea that the geographic poles could change rapidly and catastrophically is a controversial idea not widely accepted by the scientific community.

Summer 2023

Other than these two apps I haven't created anything new for more than five years. And being involved in this new line of research I hadn't updated many of the older apps. Apps that aren't updated are removed from the App Store. As a result, I'm down to eight apps at last count that remain on sale. I get the security and privacy issues, but why do I need to update an app that doesn't communicate with other apps or the cloud or use personal data?

Updating an app has become much more time-consuming. Since Apple apps must run on so many devices with different screen sizes and shapes it takes a while to generate all the required screenshots and metadata. The biggest problem for me has been the gradual abandonment of Objective-C in favor of Swift, a new language created by Apply for programming Apple devices, and only Apple devices. I don't want to invest time in Swift since I still code in C for my day job. As a result, anytime I try to do anything, figuring out how to solve even simple problems, hours become days.

Whether planned or not, with the pace of technology being what it is, obsolescence is increasing at an ever-increasing pace. Keeping up with it is exhausting even to just maintain what already exists.

Still, I can't decide if I'm in or out. I'd like to keep the option open to develop new apps since you never know what you going to need down the road, and I would like to update some old ones that Apple has removed, but as a business, I think I'm done.

Over the years, a lot of people have asked about apps for non-Apple devices. I think that re-tooling for other platforms will take even more time and effort than staying with Apple.

Then, there are web apps. Hmm, perhaps something to think about.

---

[35] Mark Carlotto, *Before Atlantis: New Evidence Suggesting the Existence of a Previous Technological Civilization on Earth*, Kindle Direct Publishers, 2018.

About the Author

Mark Carlotto has over forty years of experience in space-related applications involving remote sensing, satellite imaging, terrain mapping, pattern recognition, machine learning, and related technologies. He received a Ph.D. in Electrical Engineering from Carnegie-Mellon University in 1981 and was an assistant adjunct professor at Boston University from 1981 to 1983 where he taught courses in computer architecture and image processing.

Outside of his occupation as an engineer in the aerospace industry, in his journey as an independent scientist, Dr. Carlotto has explored a range of topics from possible extraterrestrial artifacts in our solar system, to evidence of previous technological civilizations on Earth, unidentified anomalous phenomena (UAP), and others that challenge accepted paradigms. *Diary of a Serial App Developer* is an autobiographical account of his ten-year-long stint moonlighting as an early iPhone app developer.

He can be contacted at https://markcarlotto.com.

www.ingramcontent.com/pod-product-compliance
Lightning Source LLC
LaVergne TN
LVHW060201050326
832903LV00016B/338